Sucking Steps

Safe sex How to get only pleasure from Oral sex

Jack Bracknell

THIS BOOK IS ONLY FOR ADULTS

Contents

Introduction

Oral sex is an absolutely natural continuation of the relationship of partners who love each other and one of the most delightful ways to give a bouquet of passion, tenderness, and unforgettable erotic sensations to your loved one or loved one. After all, lips and tongue are the best "tools" for sexual satisfaction of a partner who, in the process of oral caresses, will definitely reach a powerful dizzying orgasm.

You can use oral sex as a prelude to sexual intercourse, since such caresses are the most effective way to achieve the degree of arousal that is necessary for full intercourse. Sensual caresses with lips and tongue, especially mutual ones, are an excellent erotic "dessert". They allow enjoy piquant stimulation at the very end of lovemaking, reaching the peak of pleasure in this way.

But do not forget that oral caresses

bring pleasure only to loving, attentive to each other partners, and without mutual care, love passion quickly fades away. After all, only one physical intimacy is not a guarantee of a long-term relationship, even if you masterfully master the technique of oral sex and each time give partner fantastic pleasure. Show attention and care at the very beginning of your relationship. And this concerns not only finding out what your loved one (beloved) likes and dislikes in bed, but also the issue of protected sex.

SATISFACTION OF SUCKING

If you think that while satisfying each other with lips and tongues, you do not need to observe security measures, you are mistaken. The fact is that there are a number of diseases that are transmitted precisely through oral caress of the genital organs. Therefore, if you are not confident in yourself or your partner, take care of protective equipment in advance and be sure to discuss this with your loved one (beloved), jointly deciding on the most suitable condoms and latex films for both of you. After all, a huge selection of contraceptives designed specifically for oral caresses is currently presented. They protect partners from infections and at the same time do not reduce sexual pleasure in the least.

In our book you will find a description of the best ways to please each other with fellatio, cunnilingus, rimming and, of course, sex in French. You will get acquainted with modern means of protection, learn how to correctly select them depending on the techniques of oral caresses and sexual preferences.

"Super orgasm. Pleasure control panel »

Orgasm is the real culmination of a journey for two, full of daring sex experiments, daring ideas and teasing improvisation. To give a loved one an incomparable pleasure is a sensual science, the study of which should not be postponed until tomorrow.

The book will help you get to know your partner's body and your own better, tell you how to release hurricane energy in and out of bed and get unforgettable emotions from total rapprochement!

"Oral sex Secrets of explosive sensations"

To comprehend all the subtleties and techniques of sensual caresses with lips and tongue for fantastic oral sex is not at all easy.

This book will help you not only master the basics of this use arts, but also to get acquainted with new scenarios and daring ideas to stimulate the most juicy points.

"Safe sex How to get only pleasure from sex"

Thanks to the book "Safe Sex" you will learn all about modern methods of contraception and will be able to choose a reliable and most convenient method of protection for you. For sex to bring only pleasure, think about your own safety in advance and remember that the health of your loved ones depends on your health!

"How to kiss properly. The Best Guide to the Art of Kissing"

To comprehend all the subtleties and techniques of the perfect kiss is not so easy. The book "How to kiss properly" will help you not only master the basics of this art, but also raise your existing skills to incredible heights.

Daring and playful, timid and timid, passionate and burning, tender and subtle - your kisses will become unforgettable.

Fellatio

The word "fellatio" comes from the Latin fello, which means "to suck." In fact, fellatio is the oral caress of a man's genitals, which is carried out with the help of kissing, sucking, licking, and even light biting of the penis and scrotum. In most cases, the process of fellatio is accompanied by manual stimulation of the shaft of the penis.

In order for the beloved to receive incomparable pleasure, the partner should learn to caress his penis correctly. After all, oral stimulation is not such a simple process as it seems at first glance. This is a whole art, which every sensual and loving woman should master.

Varieties

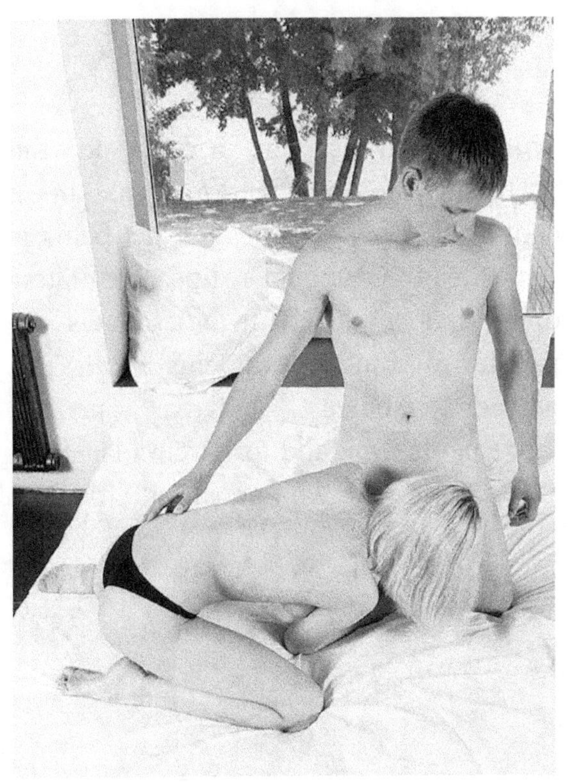

Irrumation

Irrumation is the friction in the partner's mouth. The man is in a comfortable position so that his penis is opposite the woman's lips, the latter opens her mouth wide and allows the partner to immerse the penis into it. The partner shows activity, making movements back and forth, circular, from side to side. The woman can additionally

"Tea bag"

Tea bagging is testicular caressing: the man places the testicles in the partner's open mouth and moves up and down, reminiscent of dipping a teabag into a cup.

"Melting Snow"

"Melting snow" - ejaculation in the partner's mouth. The last few seconds hold the sperm in the mouth so that it mixes with saliva, foams and increases in volume, and then allows it to drain from the parted mouth onto the chin, neck and chest. It is worth noting that this is one of the favorite plots of adult films, extremely exciting for the audience.

Technique

You are deeply mistaken if you think that sucking and licking the penis is enough for fellatio. As already noted, oral sex is a real art, having mastered it every time you will give you're loved one unforgettable moments of pleasure.

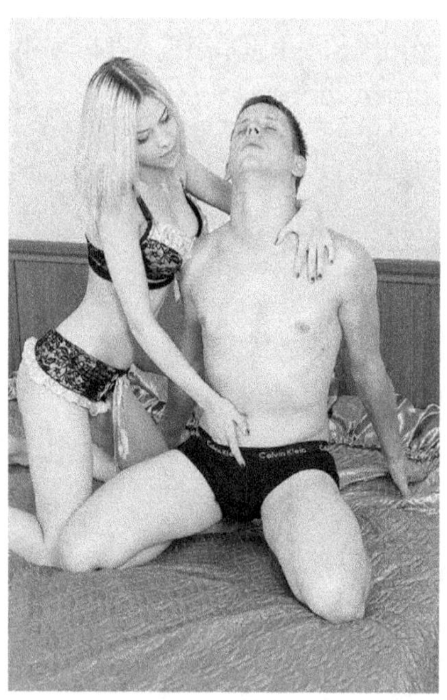

A partner will never seek sexual understanding on the side if his beloved woman learns to guess his erotic desires, excite him to the limit with virtuoso caresses of lips and tongue. Remember that for most representatives of the strong half of humanity, fellatio is a real sexual gift, fantastic pleasure and a whole sea of dizzying sensations. Therefore, if you have not yet mastered the technique of oral caresses of a penis, it's time to catch up and show your loved one what you are capable of.

If you have little or no experience with oral sex, you will need at least a superficial knowledge of male anatomy. Without them, you will not be able to competently approach the process of fellatio.

A bit about anatomy

The male reproductive organs consist of a penis, scrotum with two testicles, seminal glands, and vas deferens. The penis performs sexual functions only when erect, when the cavernous bodies located in its tissue are filled with blood. The excited member increases in length and volume, becomes hard.

STOP
CHILD
PORN!

THIS BOOK IS REGARDING TO NON MUSLIM COMMUNITY